A CATHARTI

FOR SPECIAL NEEDS PARENTS

# Working

# Through

# the

# Toughest Emotions

*A THIRTY DAY GUIDED JOURNAL*

# NANCY JONES

Working Through the Toughest Emotions

Copyright © 2020 by Nancy Jones

Printed in the United States of America

ISBN 978-1-7362709-0-5

Unapologetically Isaiah Publications LLC, New York
www.unapologeticallyisaiahpublications.com

# Hello Mama

This book was conceived at a moment when I felt quite alone. I was in the midst of my own blubbering meltdown. My son had at least one meltdown that day, and I was on my third. I had been having a rough couple of days with my son. I reluctantly called my mom to vent. Mom is great and always available, but she was stretched emotionally. She had been dealing with my brothers' medical emergency at the time. He had just undergone open heart surgery but had a stroke during the procedure. Naturally, that trumps my complaint of an oppositional child that has every room in my house looking like a tornado has passed through it. I mean, it all sounds so trivial to the person not experiencing it. I will bet you know exactly what I was feeling. If you are like any mom I know, you absolutely adore your child more than anything in the world. This makes it even more stressful when you're annoyed, angry, or having feelings of resentment. You're exhausted even after a full night's rest. That is, if you could get any rest at all. How many days have you woken up and still not felt refreshed? You go into the day on less than half a tank knowing no matter what, you will have to go those extra miles on fumes. And go you must... Yeah, that's where I was when I called Mom. School was out and I hadn't had a break from my son in weeks. Every single minute of every day without a break for weeks. Not even a bathroom break... because we take those together too.

# Hello Mama

It was so draining. He just needed so much of me, from me! I had nothing left and I was beginning to be short and mean. I was yelling, a lot. My child is perfect, but his behaviors leave a lot to be desired. At that moment, I needed more than an encouraging word. I needed someone to love me through this when I felt deflated, defeated and hopeless. My child was still bouncing off the walls, totally oblivious to my current tribulations. He was happy in his own little world. His happy world was my messy house. I needed grace and forgiveness because I was doing my best and it seemed futile. I was exhausted and everything I had to deal with was amplified. I did not realize the unrealistic expectations I had placed on myself. The trained eye would have spotted it in an instant and pulled me out of the deep.

This was an emergency. My well was empty, and I felt guilty. I was having the ugly cry moment. It was right there at that moment, I told my Mom that I wanted to help you. Yup, you! And so here we are. I promise to be transparent because I want you to know I am a real mama. I get it wrong. A lot. I have been down this block and I have hit the potholes and run into the ditch. This is about helping you see yourself and work through your emotions without judgement. You are not alone. There are many moms just like you. We feel what you are feeling. While I was uttering unintelligible words to my mom through heavy sobs, I realized I needed to be to someone the very thing that I needed.

Nancy

# Why is this so hard?

I can think of a million reasons.
What are your top ten?

## my top ten

## my top ten

Parenting my child is the hardest thing I have done in my entire life. I have literally been yelling all day long.

The demands of this life are relentless. I never get a break to collect myself.

I am exhausted all of the time.

# Day 2

How is your day going? Has it been overwhelming so far? How are you handling today's stresses?

# Day 2

Have you been yelling all day? Is the overwhelming responsibility of the day draining you?

I lost it on my child today. I totally lost it. I was so out of control. This time I was the one doing all of the screaming and yelling.

I feel horrible. I know he can't control his behavior but I can control mine. The guilt is heavy on my heart.

# Day 3

Days like this I just want to crawl under the bed and never come out. I hate when I lose control. How do you handle these days?

# Day 3

Have you ever felt like the worst parent on the block? You know the days when you lose your cool and reason goes out of the window?

I am sick and tired of people acting like I'm a bad parent because my child is having trouble controlling his emotions.

# Day 4

I cannot take the stares and the judgement doled out by so called "perfect" parents who have "perfect" children. Can you?

# Day 4

Judgement from outsiders can be harsh and difficult to swallow. How do you deal with it?

If I don't discipline him the way they think I should, I'm a bad parent.

You can't spank their challenges away.

# Day 5

My mom told me I would eventually have to "pop" my child after sitting him for just one day. She used to "pop" me when I was younger. What are your thoughts?

# Day 5

What are some of the ways your friends and family have suggested you discipline your child? Did you agree with their methods?

If one more person tells me my child does not look like he has a disability, I'm going to scream.

You can't look at a person and see their mental illness.

What does mental health look like anyway?

# Day 6

My sister told me it would be easier to give my son grace as a special needs child if he "looked like" something was wrong with him. Do you have a "normal" looking child?

# Day 6

What is normal anyway? What does normal look like? Have you ever encountered this type of attitude? How did you handle it?

Every area of my life has taken a hit, from my social life to my spiritual life.

I am not free to do anything except care for my child. My life is isolated and lonely.

I have lost contact with friends and family because they don't want to be around my child.

# Day 7

Has your life taken a hit in every area? Have you lost connections and friendships since you became a special needs parent?

# Day 7

What are some of your reasons for dropping out of the social scene you were once a part of? Were you just overwhelmed with life or did you remove yourself for another reason?

I have this nagging question in the back of my head that won't go away.

I hope I am not the cause of my child's special needs diagnosis.

Was it something I did or didn't do?

# Day 8

Do you feel like something you did or did not do is the cause for your child's disability?

# Day 8

Have you ever asked yourself that question? What in your life or history did you incorrectly attribute to your child's diagnosis?

# Day 9

I'm still trying to wrap my head around the fact that I might be taking care of my son for the rest of his life.

He may never be able to care for himself.

I'm not sure he'll ever learn to wipe his butt properly. He may never get married or go off to college.

Forever is a long time to be doing this, and there is really nothing I can do to change the struggle he is facing.

# Day 9

When you think about forever, how does it make you feel? What does your child's forever look like?

# Day 9

Do you have concerns about your future or your child's future? Have you made provisions?

It is a shame that I have to protect my child from family members.

They are mean and are always bossing him around and have even hit him when I was not around.

He is often the focus of negative attention.

# Day 10

It takes a village, but not a crazy one. How has your village responded to your child?

# Day 10

Do you feel like you are always in protective mode? Has anyone in your family ever hurt your child in or out of your presence?

# My spouse bailed on me...

# Day 11

Has your spouse or anyone in your life bailed on you; either physically or emotionally? Have you been left holding all of the responsibility?

# Day 11

Who has left you? How did you process those emotions? How did it affect your relationship with your child?

I was thrown into this war without any combat training. I was ill prepared and there were no provisions for me.

I know there is no playbook for parenting but I feel like I am living a real life version of Survivor.

# Day 12

What does your version of life look like? Are you winning or losing the Survivor Challenge?

# Day 12

Is it a minefield? It is full of potholes, ditches and stop signs that you try to navigate ? Are you getting better with time?

It's impossible to explain what goes on inside my world to a person who has not been in my shoes. They spend their time giving me advice and tips that are irrelevant to our situation.

I don't even bother.

# Day 13

Do you have anyone that you can talk to about your situation? I would imagine the only person capable of understanding is another mama in your shoes.

# Day 13

How do you handle unsolicited advice from people who don't have a clue what is going on with your child or in your world?

# Day 14

I feel like a failure...

# Day 14

Have you ever said, "I feel like a failure?" What caused you to feel that way? How did you overcome that feeling?

# Day 14

Was it something external that caused the feelings or was it your own internal processing that resulted in the feelings?

Every single aspect of my life has been changed, forever.

My life will never, ever, ever be the same.

Actually, nothing will ever be the same.

# Day 15

My life consists of therapy, evaluations, and fighting for my child. Our new normal completely erased the life I lived before.

# Day 15

What are some of the things that you mourn from your old life? Have you found peace in the new life amidst the daily chaos?

# I am in a constant state of overwhelm.

# Day 16

Some days I feel like I will explode if one more thing happens, and then it does. There is never a moment when I'm not dealing with one hundred things, all at the same time.

# Day 16

What degree of overwhelm have you been experiencing lately? Can you see yourself working through it to find some peace?

I find myself walking on eggshells. I never know what is going to happen next.

We don't get warnings, things just happen...

The **PTSD** of it all!

# Day 17

Do you find yourself walking on eggshells to prevent the next major catastrophe from happening? Is this a reality for you as well?

# Day 17

Many of us suffer from PTSD brought on by the things we face every day as special needs parents. Do you also have PTSD? Have you sought therapy for it?

I feel powerless.


I hate feeling powerless.

# Day 18

So much of what we deal with is out of our control. Can you think of a time when you felt helpless? What did you do in that situation?

# Day 18

Hindsight is 20/20. What would you have done differently in that situation? Was it something you could have controlled? Is there a way you could have maintained your power?

Today I realized that no one is coming to save me.

# Day 19

How has this sobering reality hit you? It almost took me out, but then I adjusted. How did you deal with this realization?

# Day 19

Is there anyone in your circle or among your mama friends who supports you in a meaningful way? How does this make you feel?

Caring for my child is all-consuming. I have all but lost myself.

I don't know who I am anymore.

# Day 20

Have you lost yourself in the auto-pilot life you lead? What do you miss most about you? What has changed about the woman you used to be?

# Day 20

Do you make time for yourself? Is that even a possibility? I know for me, time is a premium and so little of it belongs to just me. How about you?

The time I spend advocating for my child is equivalent to having a second full-time job.

# Day 21

How much of your life has been consumed by advocating for your child? The endless meetings and unfruitful time spent on the phone.

# Day 21

I had to leave my full-time job to properly care of my child. Can you work a job and keep up? Are you constantly being interrupted at work?

I thought about bringing a box of donuts to the advocacy meeting but I'm probably going to be raising hell in there. I think I'll just put my game face on instead.

# Day 22

I used to go to the advocacy meeting with high hopes that those in charge would be willing to help me. I expected them to bend over backwards to help me. That is the reason they are there.

# Day 22

Being nice in advocacy meetings doesn't work for me. When I do that, they run all over me and I end up getting nothing we need. What worked for you?

# Some days I hate my life...

# Day 23

Shhh... Someone might hear me say that and JUDGE ME! I don't hate life or living, it's just that I don't love the struggle and stress of it all. It's constant...and daily... and I'm over it!

# Day 23

When was the last time you said this? Have you ever been brave enough to say it out loud? How are you feeling about your life today?

A stranger approached me today with her two cents. She began to say "If that was my child..."

I cut her off... THIS IS NOT YOUR CHILD!

People can be such jerks!

# Day 24

I can't tell you how many times this has happened to me. People are really ballsy and entitled sometimes and feel they have the right to speak in such situations.

# Day 24

I've wanted to tell people "don't help me" because they don't know the first thing about what is going on. How do you handle it?

# I can't remember the last day we didn't have some sort of catastrophe.

# Day 25

When was the last catastrophe? What happened? Walk through the feeling of that day. How did you handle it? Did it catch you off guard?

# Day 25

When was your last peaceful day? Can you even remember the last day you had peace from morning until night?

I'm giving all of me and I feel like I won't last much longer.

# Day 26

How are you feeling at this very moment? What is you biggest concern? Is there anyone you could call upon to help lighten your load? For many of us the answer is "no." That is our harsh reality and leads to burnout.

# Day 26

What ways have you identified to keep from burning out? How do you recharge? Can you get up an hour early and just do something for you?

I have missed out on so many life events because the current emergency was my child.

Making plans is a thing of the past. We probably won't make it anyway.

# Day 27

My my best friend was starring in a Christmas play. I was so excited to hear her sing and act. We were almost to the door when it happened. Major meltdown. I had to catch it on video. Such is my life.

# Day 27

What was the major event that you missed or is it that you just stopped taking invitations because this type of thing happens all the time.

# The dreams I have for my child and the reality that he is living are completely different.

# Day 28

What dreams do you have for your child that might not be realized because of their disability? Does it make you sad to think about it?

# Day 28

What reality is your child living? Have you taken the time to mourn that reality? How do you feel when others are bragging on their children knowing your child will never do those things?

People outside our immediate family love my child more than those who are closest to us.

We love who loves us.

When you have a special needs child you are ostracized.

We have learned to take love wherever it comes from.

# Day 29

Has your family ostracized you because of your child or have they become distant and unwelcoming? How does it make you feel?

# Day 29

There are those who will see beauty in your child. Have you identified those people in your life? How has that made you feel about love and what it truly means to be family?

Who is going to take care of my child if something happens to me?

Who is going to care for him like I do?

Who is even going to want that responsibility?

# Day 30

I've asked many mamas and this is, by far, their greatest concern. How about you? Do you have a plan in place?

# Day 30

Who is the person you would trust with your child? Have your identified anyone who would take on the awesome challenge of raising them? How much stress do you feel around this topic?

# A Final Word

This IS hard! However, you are doing an exceptional job parenting your child, no matter what it feels like. I'm sure you can attest to the fact that your child loves you and forgives everything you think you may have done wrong. Your are their one and only Super Woman. Be strong and stay in the fight. The one true mark of a superhero is that no matter how many times you get hit, you get back up again. We have no choice. My prayer is that you know you are loved and wanted and specifically created for your little one to love and guide them through this life. No matter what comes your way, you are fully equipped to handle it. I believe in you. Your child is looking to you for all you've got to give. Give it liberally and they will return it to you in love. You've got this!

xoxo Nancy

Made in the USA
Monee, IL
15 April 2022

94808092R00056